# THE MAN WITHOUT A
# COUNTRY

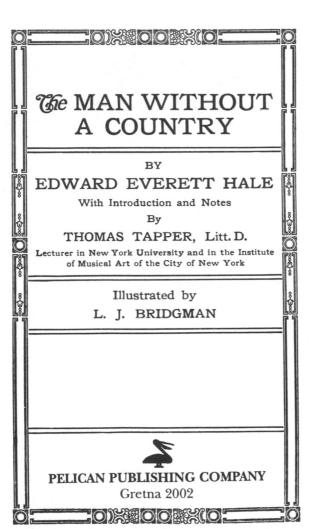

# The MAN WITHOUT A COUNTRY

BY

## EDWARD EVERETT HALE

With Introduction and Notes

By

## THOMAS TAPPER, Litt. D.

Lecturer in New York University and in the Institute
of Musical Art of the City of New York

Illustrated by

## L. J. BRIDGMAN

PELICAN PUBLISHING COMPANY
Gretna 2002

Copyright © 1917
By The Page Company

First edition, July 1917
First Pelican edition, July 2002

**Library of Congress Cataloging-in-Publication Data**

Hale, Edward Everett, 1822-1909.
  The man without a country / Edward Everett Hale. A message to
Garcia / Elbert Hubbard—1st Pelican ed.
    p. cm.
  ISBN 1-56554-453-6 (alk. paper)
   1. Burr Conspiracy, 1805-1807—Fiction. 2. Stateless persons—
Fiction. 3. Soldiers—Fiction. 4. Exiles—Fiction. 5. Rowan, Andrew
Summers. 6. Spanish-American War, 1898. 7. Success. I. Hubbard,
Elbert, 1856-1915. Message to Garcia. 2002. II. Title: Message to
Garcia. III. Title.

PS1772 .M3 2002
813'.4—dc21                                      2002027061

Printed in the United States of America

Published by Pelican Publishing Company, Inc.
1000 Burmaster Street, Gretna, Louisiana 70053

" Old Glory "

# FOREWORD.

.

---

THE author of " The Man Without a Country "
has taken pains specifically to inform his readers
of the purpose that actuated him in writing the
story of Philip Nolan. Although this Philip Nolan
is a purely fictitious character, he was created for
a definite object, namely, to teach young Americans
what it means to have a country.

The story lays before us in a singularly vivid
manner the duty we owe our country. It insists
that our sense of duty shall be an abiding convic-
tion which shall blossom into loyalty and power;
the loyalty fragrant with the love of the home land;
the power springing from the impulse to defend it.

In the frenzy of an unguarded moment, Philip
Nolan exclaimed: " I wish that I may never hear
of the United States again." To his utter astonish-
ment and life-long grief his wish was granted!

Old Morgan, who was holding court, heard him with amazement. It took but a quarter of an hour to determine the sentence.

" Prisoner, hear the sentence of the Court!"

One can hear the voice of Old Morgan, a voice choking with sorrow, and yet fired with suppressed indignation, as it announced:

" The Court decides, subject to the approval of the President, that you never hear the name of the United States again."

Nolan laughed, the author continues.

But we do not find that he ever laughed again. Not until the end of his days, when he lay dying, do we read of the blessed smile that crept over his white face.

How that wish, how that exclamation of a hot-headed youth: " I wish that I may never hear of the United States again!" echoed back to him. As he wandered on the sea it reached him from north and south, from east and west. It cried to him in every breeze, in every break of a whitecap wave. And not alone did the wish sound upon the ear its awful reminder. It did more — and cruelly. It darkened his eyes to things he might not see. It stilled his tongue to words he might not utter. It closed his ears to words he might not hear. It palsied his hands that he might not raise them in supplication to the land of his birth. Oh, Philip Nolan! What man, in the utterance of a few simple words, ever before brought down upon himself so heavy a punishment?

And yet, Philip Nolan is a lovable character. No man can read his words, beginning " O Danforth, I know I am dying," with eyes undimmed. A noble soul speaks through a body that was cruelly imprisoned, though justly enough, as he, himself, would have said. Never a complaint came from his lips; but many a gentle word. No act of his was ever calculated to do harm or to cause pain: but many a kind and loving deed did he perform. We follow him year after year, watching him adjust himself to his life imprisonment; and we witness, strange to say, not the distress of a man who suffers, but somewhat of the joy of a man who is finding himself.

The Philip Nolan who was condemned by Old Morgan passes from our ken and a new Philip Nolan is born; a new Philip Nolan who could de-

clare from a clean heart as he lay on his death-
bed:

"There cannot be a man who loves the old flag
as I do, or prays for it as I do, or hopes for it as
I do."

The imagery of the story is vivid. The reader's
interest is sustained at a high pitch, for at every
turn of the narrative a fresh dramatic incident
grips the attention. Nearly every page is rich in
allusions to places, people and historical events.
Although the story takes its inception in a small
military court room, it seems to embrace the whole
world ere its reverberations die away.

The author was born in Boston, April 23, 1822.
His father, who was active in the business life of
Boston, founded the *Daily Advertiser*. He was
Nathan Hale, and related to the patriot of that
name. The mother was Sarah Preston Everett,
sister of Edward Everett, the orator, and for him
the boy was named.

Edward Everett Hale was graduated from Har-
vard in 1839, at the age of seventeen. He spent
two years as teacher of Latin in the Boston Latin

School, and then took up the study of theology. His first important ministerial charge was at Worcester, Mass. Thence he went, in 1856, to the South Congregational Church in Boston, where he remained for forty-four years, until 1900. During the remaining years of his life he was Chaplain to the United States Senate. Doctor Hale died June 10, 1909, in Roxbury, Mass.

Doctor Hale began to write early in life. He excelled in the short story form, of which this book is, perhaps, his most significant example; although another, entitled "Ten Times Ten," was so warmly received that it inspired the founding of the Lend-a-Hand Society.

THOMAS TAPPER.

# PREFACE.

~~~~~~

IT is difficult for young readers of the present generation to understand or to imagine what was the condition of public feeling in many parts of the United States, at different periods in the Civil War, which lasted from 1861 to 1865.

In the year 1863, a great deal of distrust expressed itself, even in some of the northern states, as to whether it were worth while for the North to make the sacrifices it was making. In the state of Ohio, a prominent statesman expressed himself with such contempt as to the national government, that General Burnside, who was in command of the national army in that region, sent him over the lines to the rebels, saying that he seemed to belong with them, rather than in his own country. It was in that summer that I wrote the story which is in the reader's hands. My wish was simply the wish to show what one's Country is, and what her claims are, without any reference to any of the other questions which were involved in the Civil War. I tried to interest my readers in a hero of whom they should know little, except that he had no country, having forfeited the birth-right which all other men have.

To give this hero a name, and to surround him with circumstances which were in the least probable, I connected him with the movement, still mysterious, of Aaron Burr, near the beginning of this century. I supposed him to be an officer of the army of the country which he disowned. And, in the slight historical references to Burr and his undertaking, whatever it was, which will be found in the beginning, I followed the truth of history.

I wanted a name for the hero which was familiar at that time in the Southwest. I remembered a young man, named Nolan, who was the correspondent and friend of James Wilkinson, who was the general in command

of the United States army at the time Burr
was arrested.  James Wilkinson was a traitor
to his country; and a traitor to Burr also, as
I believe.  That is, I think that he had given
Burr encouragement that he would join him
in his plan, whatever it was.  But when the
moment came, he took measures for the arrest of Burr, and disowned him.  With that
matter, however, this story has nothing to do.
In seeking a name for my hero, I remembered
Wilkinson's correspondent, Nolan, and, as it
happened, I thought his name was " Stephen
Nolan."  He is so spoken of in my story, and
the reader will find that the hero of this book
alludes to Stephen Nolan and to his death in
Texas.

Long after the story was first published, I
found that the real name of the true Nolan
was Philip, not Stephen.  He was an adven-
turer, who was killed near Waco, in Texas, by
the Spaniards in 1801.  I had made a mistake
in calling him Stephen, and I had transferred
his name, to be the name of the imaginary
person whom I had created.  To this care-

lessness or accident, I have owed a large correspondence, very interesting and instructive to me, with the relatives of the real " Philip Nolan " and others. I have his portrait, as it was painted in a miniature for the lady whom he married. In another book, called " Philip Nolan's Friends," I have given truly the outlines of his tragic history. But his connection with my Philip Nolan was a mere accident. The Philip Nolan of the book in the reader's hands is an imaginary character, who was created for the single purpose of teaching young Americans what it is to have a country, what is the duty which they owe to that country, and how central that duty is among all the duties of their lives. I was glad to find, when the story was published, that this moral was appreciated. I have many letters, which I prize highly, from persons who were before strangers to me, who read it in dreary watches at sea, or by the light of camp-fires on shore, when they were risking their lives for the country which had the right to claim their service, and which did not assert that right in vain.   I have a memorandum of the death of " Philip Nolan," a black man from Lousiana, to whom that war gave a country, and who laid down his life for her on the banks of the James River.   I suppose that this " Philip Nolan " was named from the same Philip Nolan who gave a name to my hero. I have had the pleasure of knowing that my Philip Nolan has made many friends in all parts of this nation.   And now that the story is printed as a school-book, I dedicate it to the boys and girls who also are citizens of the United States, with the hope which Philip Nolan expressed to Frederick Ingham when he was a midshipman, and with the injunction which he gave to that boy:—

" For your country, boy, and for that flag, never dream a dream but of serving her, as she bids you, though the service carry you through a thousand hells.   No matter what happens to you, no matter who flatters you or who abuses you, never look at another flag; never let a night pass but you pray God to bless that flag.   Remember, boy, that behind all these men you have to do with, behind officers and government, the people even, there is the Country Herself, your Country, and that you belong to Her, as you belong to your own mother. Stand by Her, boy, as you would stand by your mother, if those devils there had got hold of her today. O if anybody had said so to me when I was your age!"

EDWARD EVERETT HALE.

# ILLUSTRATIONS.

# THE MAN WITHOUT A COUNTRY.[1]*

~~~~~~~~

I SUPPOSE[2] that very few casual readers of the *New York Herald* of August 13th observed, in an obscure corner among the "Deaths," the announcement,—

"NOLAN. Died, on board U. S. Corvette[3] Levant, Lat. 2° 11′ S., Long. 131° W., on the 11th of May, PHILIP NOLAN."

I happened to observe it, because I was stranded at the old Mission-House in Mackinaw,[4] waiting for a Lake Superior steamer which did not choose to come, and I was devouring to the very stubble all the current literature I could get hold of, even down to the deaths and marriages in the *Herald*. My memory for names and people is good, and the reader will see, as he goes on, that I had reason enough to remember Philip Nolan. There are hundreds of readers who would have paused at that announcement, if the officer of the Levant who reported it had chosen to make it thus :—" Died, May 11th, THE MAN WITHOUT A COUNTRY."

For it was as "The Man without a Country" that poor Philip Nolan had generally been known by the officers who had him in charge during some fifty years, as, indeed, by all men who sailed under them. I dare say there is many a man who has taken wine with him once a fortnight, in a three years' cruise, who never knew that his name was "Nolan," or whether the poor wretch had any name at all.

There can now be no possible harm in telling this poor creature's story. Reason enough there has been till now, ever since Madison's[1] administration went out in 1817, for very strict secrecy, the secrecy of honor itself, among the gentlemen of the navy who have had Nolan in successive charge. And certainly it speaks well for the *esprit de corps*[2] of the profession, and the personal honor of its members, that to the press this man's story has been wholly unknown, —and, I think, to the country at large also. I have reason to think, from some investigations I made in the Naval Archives[3] when I was attached to the Bureau of Construction, that every official report relating to him was burned when Ross[4] burned the public buildings at Washington. One of the Tuckers, or possibly one of the Watsons, had Nolan in charge at the end of the war; and when, on returning from his cruise, he reported at Washington to one of the Crowninshields,—who was in the Navy Department when he came home,—he found that the Department ignored the whole business. Whether they really knew nothing about it or whether it was a "*Non mi recordo*"[1] determined on as a piece of policy, I do not know. But this I do know, that since 1817, and possibly before, no naval officer has mentioned Nolan in his report of a cruise.

But, as I say, there is no need for secrecy any longer. And now the poor creature is dead, it seems to me worth while to tell a little of his story, by way of showing young Americans[2] of today what it is to be A MAN WITHOUT A COUNTRY.

Philip Nolan was as fine a young officer as there was in the "Legion of the West," as the Western division of our army was then called. When Aaron Burr[3] made his first dashing expedition down to New Orleans in 1805, at Fort Massac[4] or somewhere above on the river, he met, as the Devil would have it, this gay, dashing, bright young fellow, at some dinner-party, I think. Burr marked him, talked to him, walked with him, took him a day or two's voyage in his flat-boat, and, in short, fascinated him. For the next year, barrack-life[5] was very tame to poor Nolan. He occasionally availed

himself of the permission the great man had
given him to write to him.   Long, high-worded,
stilted letters the poor boy wrote and rewrote
and copied.   But never a line did he have in
reply from the gay deceiver.   The other boys
in the garrison sneered at him, because he sac-
rificed in this unrequited affection for a politician
the time which they devoted to Monongahela,[1]
hazard,[2] and high-low-jack.[3]   Bourbon,[4] euchre,
and poker[5] were still unknown.   But one day
Nolan had his revenge.   This time Burr came
down the river not as an attorney seeking a
place for his office, but as a disguised conqueror.
He had defeated I know not how many district-
attorneys; he had dined at I know not how
many public dinners; he had been heralded in
I know not how many *Weekly Arguses*,[6] and it
was rumored that he had an army behind him
and an empire before him.   It was a great day
·—his arrival—to poor Nolan.   Burr had not
been at the fort an hour before he sent for him.
That evening he asked Nolan to take him out
in his skiff, to show him a canebrake[7] or a cotton-
wood tree, as he said,—really to seduce him;
and by the time the sale was over, Nolan was
enlisted body and soul.   From that time, though
he did not yet know it, he lived as A MAN WITH-
OUT A COUNTRY.

What Burr meant to do I know no more than

you, dear reader.  It is none of our business just now.  Only, when the grand catastrophe came, and Jefferson[1] and the House of Virginia of that day undertook to break on the wheel[2] all the possible Clarences of the then House of York[3] by the great treason-trial at Richmond, some of the lesser fry in that distant Mississippi Valley, which was farther from us than Puget's Sound[4] is today, introduced the like novelty on their provincial stage, and, to while away the monotony of the summer at Fort Adams[5] got up, for *spectacles*, a string of court-martials[6] on the officers there.  One and another of the colonels and majors were tried, and, to fill out the list, little Nolan, against whom, Heaven knows, there was evidence enough,—that he was sick of the service, had been willing to be false to it, and would have obeyed any order to march any-whither with any one who would follow him had the order been signed, "By command of His Exc. A. Burr."  The courts dragged on.  The big flies escaped,—rightly for all I know.  Nolan was proved guilty enough, as I say; yet you and I would never have heard of him, reader, but that, when the president of the court asked him at the close, whether he wished to say anything to show that he had always been faithful to the United States, he cried out, in a fit of frenzy,—

"D—n the United States! I wish I may never hear of the United States again!"

I suppose he did not know how the words shocked old Colonel Morgan,[1] who was holding the court. Half the officers who sat in it had served through the Revolution, and their lives, not to say their necks, had been risked for the very idea which he so cavalierly cursed in his madness. He, on his part, had grown up in the West of those days, in the midst of "Spanish plot," "Orleans plot,"[2] and all the rest. He had been educated on a plantation where the finest company was a Spanish officer or a French merchant from Orleans. His education, such as it was, had been perfected in commercial expeditions to Vera Cruz,[3] and I think he told me his father once hired an Englishman to be a private tutor for a winter on the plantation. He had spent half his youth with an older brother, hunting horses in Texas; and, in a word, to him "United States" was scarcely a reality. Yet he had been fed by "United States" for all the years since he had been in the army. He had sworn on his faith as a Christian to be true to "United States." It was "United States" which gave him the uniform he wore, and the sword by his side. Nay, my poor Nolan, it was only because "United States" had picked you out first as one of her own confidential men of

"'I WISH I MAY NEVER HEAR OF THE UNITED STATES
AGAIN.'"

honor that "A. Burr" cared for you a straw more than for the flat-boat men who sailed his ark for him. I do not excuse Nolan ; I only explain to the reader why he damned his country, and wished he might never hear her name again.

He never did hear her name but once again[1] From that moment, September 23, 1807, till the day he died, May 11, 1863, he never heard her name again. For that half century and more he was a man without a country.

Old Morgan, as I said, was terribly shocked. If Nolan had compared George Washington to Benedict Arnold[2], or had cried, "God save King George[3]," Morgan would not have felt worse. He called the court[4] into his private room, and returned in fifteen minutes, with a face like a sheet, to say,—

"Prisoner, hear the sentence of the Court! The court decides, subject to the approval of the President, that you never hear the name of the United States again."

Nolan laughed. But nobody else laughed. Old Morgan was too solemn, and the whole room was hushed dead as night for a minute. Even Nolan lost his swagger in a moment. Then Morgan added,—

"Mr Marshal[5], take the prisoner to Orleans in an armed boat, and deliver him to the naval commander there."

The Marshal gave his orders and the prisoner was taken out of court.

" Mr. Marshal," continued old Morgan, " see that no one mentions the United States to the prisoner. Mr. Marshal, make my respects to Lieutenant Mitchell at Orleans, and request him to order that no one shall mention the United States to the prisoner while he is on board ship. You will receive your written orders from the officer on duty here this evening. The court is adjourned without day!"

I have always supposed that Colonel Morgan himself took the proceedings of the court to Washington City, and explained them to Mr. Jefferson. Certain it is that the President approved them,— certain, that is, if I may believe[2] the men who say they have seen his signature. Before the Nautilus got round from New Orleans to the Northern Atlantic coast with the prisoner on board the sentence had been approved, and he was a man without a country.

The plan then adopted was substantially the same which was necessarily followed ever after. Perhaps it was suggested by the necessity of sending him by water from Fort Adams and Orleans. The Secretary of the Navy — it must have been the first Crowninshield[3] though he is a man I do not remember — was requested to put Nolan on board a government vessel bound on a long cruise, and to direct that he should be only so far confined there as to make it certain that he never saw or heard of the country. We had few long cruises then, and the navy was very much out of favor; and as almost all of this story is traditional, as I have explained, I do not know certainly what his first cruise was. But the commander to whom he was intrusted, — perhaps it was Tingey[1] or Shaw, though I think it was one of the younger men, — we are all old enough now, — regulated the etiquette[2] and the precautions of the affair, and according to his scheme they were carried out, I suppose, till Nolan died.

When I was second officer of the Intrepid, some thirty years after, I saw the original paper of instructions. I have been sorry ever since that I did not copy the whole of it. It ran, however, much in this way : —

"WASHINGTON (with a date, which must have been late in 1807).

"SIR, — You will receive from Lieutenant Neale the person of Philip Nolan, late a Lieutenant in the United States Army.

"This person on his trial by court-martial 'expressed with an oath the wish that he might never hear of the United States again.'

"The court sentenced him to have his wish fulfilled.

" For the present, the execution of the order is intrusted by the President to this Department.

" You will take the prisoner on board your ship, and keep him there with such precautions as shall prevent his escape.

" You will provide him with such quarters,[1] rations,[2] and clothing as would be proper for an officer of his late rank, if he were a passenger on your vessel on the business of his Government.

" The gentlemen on board will make any arrangements agreeable to themselves regarding his society. He is to be exposed to no indignity of any kind, nor is he ever unnecessarily to be reminded that he is a prisoner.

" But under no circumstances is he ever to hear of his country or to see any information regarding it; and you will specially caution all the officers under your command to take care, that, in the various indulgences which may be granted, this rule, in which his punishment is involved, shall not be broken.

" It is the intention of the Government that he shall never again see the country which he has disowned. Before the end of your cruise you will receive orders which will give effect to this intention.

" Respectfully yours,

" W. SOUTHWARD,

**For the Secretary of the Navy.''**

If I had only preserved the whole of this paper, there would be no break in the beginning of my sketch of this story. For Captain Shaw, if it were he, handed it to his successor in the charge, and he to his, and I suppose the commander of the Levant has it to-day as his authority for keeping this man in this mild custody.

The rule adopted on board the ships on which I have met "the man without a country" was, I think, transmitted from the beginning. No mess liked to have him permanently, because his presence cut off all talk of home or of the prospect of return, of politics or letters, of peace or of war,— cut off more than half the talk men liked to have at sea. But it was always thought too hard that he should never meet the rest of us, except to touch hats, and we finally sank into one system. He was not permitted to talk with the men, unless an officer was by. With officers he had unrestrained intercourse, as far as they and he chose. But he grew shy, though he had favorites: I was one. Then the captain always asked him to dinner on Monday. Every mess in succession took up the invitation in its turn. According to the size of the ship, you had him at your mess more or less often at dinner. His breakfast he ate in his own state-room, —

he always had a state-room, — which was where
a sentinel[1] or somebody on the watch could see
the door.    And whatever else he ate or drank,
he ate or drank alone.    Sometimes, when the
marines or sailors had any special jollification,
they were permitted to invite " Plain Buttons,"
as they called him.    Then Nolan was sent with
some officer, and the men were forbidden to
speak of home while he was there.    I believe
the theory was that the sight of his punishment
did them good.    They called him " Plain Buttons," because while he always chose to wear
a regulation army-uniform, he was not permitted
to wear the army-button, for the reason that it
bore either the initials or the insignia of the
country he had disowned.

I remember, soon after I joined the navy, I
was on shore with some of the older officers
from our ship and from the Brandywine, which
we had met at Alexandria.[2]    We had leave to
make a party and go up to Cairo[3] and the Pyra-
mids.    As we jogged along (you went on don-
keys then), some of the gentlemen (we boys
called them " Dons,[4]" but the phrase was long
since changed) fell to talking about Nolan, and
some one told the system which was adopted
from the first about his books and other reading.
As he was almost never permitted to go on
shore, even though the vessel lay in port for

months, his time at the best hung heavy; and
everybody was permitted to lend him books, if
they were not published in America and made
no allusion to it.   These were common enough
in the old days, when people in the other hemi-
sphere talked of the United States as little as
we do of Paraguay.   He had almost all the foreign papers that came into the ship, sooner or
later; only somebody must go over them first,
and cut out any advertisement or stray para-
graph that alluded to America.   This was a
little cruel sometimes, when the back of what
was cut out might be as innocent as Hesiod![1]
Right in the midst of one of Napoleon's battles,
or one of Canning's speeches,[2] poor Nolan would
find a great hole, because on the back of the
page of that paper there had been an advertisement of a packet[3] for New York, or a scrap from
the President's message.   I say this was the
first time I ever heard of this plan, which afterwards I had enough and more than enough to
do with.   I remember it, because poor Phillips,
who was of the party, as soon as the allusion to
reading was made, told a story of something
which happened at the Cape of Good Hope on
Nolan's first voyage; and it is the only thing I
ever knew of that voyage.   They had touched
at the Cape, and had done the civil thing with
the English Admiral and the fleet, and then,

leaving for a long cruise up the Indian Ocean, Phillips had borrowed a lot of English books from an officer, which, in those days, as indeed in these, was quite a windfall. Among them, as the Devil would order, was the "Lay of the Last Minstrel," which they had all of them heard of, but which most of them had never seen. I think it could not have been published long. Well, nobody thought there could be any risk of anything national in that, though Phillips swore old Shaw had cut out the "Tempest"" from Shakespeare before he let Nolan have it, because he said "the Bermudas ought to be ours, and, by Jove, should be one day." So Nolan was permitted to join the circle one afternoon when a lot of them sat on deck smoking and reading aloud. People do not do such things so often now; but when I was young we got rid of a great deal of time so. Well, so it happened that in his turn Nolan took the book and read to the others; and he read very well, as I know. Nobody in the circle knew a line of the poem, only it was all magic and Border chivalry,³ and was ten thousand years ago. Poor Nolan read steadily through the fifth canto, stopped a minute and drank something, and then began, without a thought of what was coming,——

　　" Breathes there the man, with soul so dead,
　　Who never to himself hath said,"——

It seems impossible to us that anybody ever
heard this for the first time; but all these fellows did then, and poor Nolan himself went on,
still unconsciously or mechanically, —

　　" This is my own, my native land ! "

Then they all saw something was to pay; but
he expected to get through, I suppose, turned a
little pale, but plunged on,—

　　" Whose heart hath ne'er within him burned,
　　　As home his footsteps he hath turned
　　　　From wandering on a foreign strand ? —
　　　If such there breathe, go, mark him well,"–

By this time the men were all beside themselves, wishing there was any way to make him
turn over two pages; but he had not quite
presence of mind for that; he gagged a little,
colored crimson, and staggered on, —

　　" For him no minstrel raptures swell ;
　　　High though his titles, proud his name,
　　　Boundless his wealth as wish can claim,
　　　Despite these titles,˙power, and pelf,
　　　The wretch, concentred all in self," —

and here the poor fellow choked, could not go
on, but started up, swung the book into the sea,
vanished into his state-room, "And by Jove,"
said Philips, "we did not see him for two months
again. And I had to make up some beggarly

story to that English surgeon why I did not return his Walter Scott to him."

That story shows about the time when Nolan's braggadocio[1] must have broken down. At first, they said he took a very high tone, considered his imprisonment a mere farce, affected to enjoy the voyage, and all that; but Phillips said that after he came out of his state-room he never was the same man again. He never read aloud again, unless it was the Bible or Shakespeare or something else he was sure of. But it was not that merely. He never entered in with the other young men exactly as a companion again. He was always shy afterwards, when I knew him, — very seldom spoke, unless he was spoken to, except to a very few friends. He lighted up occasionally, — I remember late in his life hearing him fairly eloquent on something which had been suggested to him by one of Fléchier's sermons,[2] — but generally he had the nervous, tired look of a heart-wounded man.

When Captain Shaw was coming home, — if as I say, it was Shaw — rather to the surprise of everybody, they made one of the Windward Islands,[3] and lay off and on for nearly a week. The boys said the officers were sick of salt-junk,[4] and meant to have turtle-soup before they came home. But after several days the Warren came to the same rendezvous;[5] they exchanged signals; she sent to Phillips and these home-ward bound men, letters and papers and told them she was outward-bound, perhaps to the Mediterranean, and took poor Nolan and his traps on the boat back to try his second cruise. He looked very blank when he was told to get ready to join her. He had known enough of the signs of the sky to know that till that moment he was going "home." But this was a distinct evidence of something he had not thought of, perhaps, — that there was no going home for him, even to a prison. And this was the first of some twenty such transfers, which brought him sooner or later into half our best vessels, but which kept him all his life at least some hundred miles from the country he had hoped he might never hear of again.

It may have been on that second cruise, — it was once when he was up the Mediterranean, — that Mrs. Graff, the celebrated Southern beauty of those days danced with him. They had been lying a long time in the Bay of Naples, and the officers were very intimate in the English fleet, and there had been great festivities, and our men thought they must give a great ball on board the ship. How they ever did it on board the Warren I am sure I do not know. Perhaps it was not the Warren, or perhaps ladies did not take up so much room as they do now. They wanted to use Nolan's state-room for something, and they hated to do it without asking him to the ball; so the captain said they might ask him, if they would be responsible that he did not talk with the wrong people, "who would give him intelligence." So the dance went on, the finest party that had ever been known, I dare say; for I never heard of a man-of-war ball that was not. For ladies they had the family of the American consul, one or two travellers, who had adventured so far, and a nice bevy[1] of English girls and matrons, perhaps[2] Lady Hamilton[3] herself.

Well, different officers relieved each other in standing and talking with Nolan in a friendly way, so as to be sure that nobody else spoke to him. The dancing went on with spirit, and after a while even the fellows who took this honorary guard of Nolan ceased to fear any *contretemps*.[4] Only when some English lady — Lady Hamilton, as I said, perhaps — called for a set of "American dances," an odd thing happened. Everybody then danced contra-dances.[5] The black band, nothing loath, conferred as to what "American dances" were, and started off with "Virginia Reel," which they followed with "Money Musk," which, in its turn in those days, should have been followed by "The Old Thirteen."[6] But just as Dick, the leader, tapped

for his fiddles to begin, and bent forward, about
to say, in true negro state, "'The Old Thirteen,' gentlemen and ladies!" as he had said
"'Virginny Reel,' if you please!" and "'Money-
Musk,' if you please!" the captain's boy tapped
him on the shoulder, whispered to him, and he
did not announce the name of the dance; he
merely bowed, began on the air, and they all
fell to,— the officers teaching the English girls
the figure, but not telling them why it had no
name.

But that is not the story I started to tell.—
As the dancing went on, Nolan and our fellows
all got at ease, as I said,— so much so, that it
seemed quite natural for him to bow to that
splendid Mrs. Graff, and say,—

"I hope you have not forgotten me, Miss
Rutledge.   Shall I have the honor of dancing?"

He did it so quickly, that Fellows, who was
by him, could not hinder him.   She laughed
and said,—

"I am not Miss Rutledge any longer, Mr.
Nolan; but I will dance all the same," just nod-
ded to Fellows, as if to say he must leave Mr.
Nolan to her, and led him off to the place where
the dance was forming.

Nolan thought he had got his chance.   He
had known her at Philadelphia, and at other
places had met her, and this was a Godsend.

You could not talk in contra-dances as you do in cotillions, or even in the pauses of waltzing; but there were chances for tongues and sounds, as well as for eyes and blushes. He began with her travels, and Europe, and Vesuvius², and the French; and then, when they had worked down, and had that long talking-time at the bottom of the set, he said, boldly,— a little pale, she said, as she told me the story, years after,—

"And what do you hear from home, Mrs. Graff?"

And that splendid creature looked through him. Jove! how she must have looked through him!

"Home!! Mr. Nolan!!! I thought you were the man who never wanted to hear of home again!"— and she walked directly up the deck to her husband, and left poor Nolan alone, as he always was. He did not dance again.

I cannot give any history of him in order; nobody can now; and, indeed, I am not trying to. These are the traditions, which I sort out, as I believe them, from the myths which have been told about this man for forty years. The lies that have been told about him are legion. The fellows used to say he was the "Iron Mask³"; and poor George Pons went to his grave in the belief that this was the author of "Junius⁴," who was being punished for his cele-

"'AND WHAT DO YOU HEAR FROM HOME, MRS. GRAFF?'"

brated libel on Thomas Jefferson. Pons was
not very strong in the historical line.  A hap-
pier story than either of these I have told is of
the War.   That came along soon after.   I have
heard this affair told in three or four ways,—
and, indeed, it may have happened more than
once.   But which ship it was on I cannot tell.
However, in one, at least, of the great frigate-
duels with the English, in which the navy was
really baptized, it happened that a round-shot
from the enemy entered one of our ports square,
and took right down the officer of the gun himself, and almost every man of the gun's crew.
Now you may say what you choose about cour-
age, but that is not a nice thing to see.   But, as
the men who were not killed picked themselves
up, and as they and the surgeon's people were
carrying off the bodies, there appeared Nolan, in
his shirt sleeves, with the rammer in his hand,
and, just as if he had been an officer, told them
off with authority,— who should go to the cock-
pit with the wounded men, who should stay with
him,— perfectly cheery, and with that way which
makes men feel sure all is right and is going to
be right.   And he finished loading his gun with
his own hands, aimed it, and bade the men fire.
And there he stayed, captain of that gun, keeping those fellows in spirits, till the enemy struck,
— sitting on the carriage while the gun was

cooling, though he was exposed all the time,—
showing them easier ways to handle heavy shot,
— making the raw hands' laugh at their own
blunders,— and when the gun cooled again, getting it loaded and fired twice as often as any
other gun on the ship.   The captain walked forward by way of encouraging the men, and Nolan
touched his hat, and said,—

" I am showing them how we do this in the
artillery, sir."

And this is the part of the story where all
the legends agree; and the Commodore said,—

" I see you do, and I thank you, sir; and I
shall never forget this day, sir; and you never
shall, sir."

And after the whole thing was over, and he
had the Englishman's sword, in the midst of the
state and ceremony of the quarter-deck, he
said,—

" Where is Mr. Nolan?   Ask Mr. Nolan to
come here."

And when Nolan came, the captain said,—

" Mr. Nolan, we are all very grateful to you
today; you are one of us today; you will be
named in the despatches."

And then the old man took off his own sword
of ceremony, and gave it to Nolan, and made
him put it on.   The man told me this who saw
it.   Nolan cried like a baby, and well he might.

"'I SHALL NEVER FORGET THIS DAY, SIR.'"

He had not worn a sword since that infernal day at Fort Adams. But always afterwards, on occasions of ceremony, he wore that quaint old French sword of the Commodore's.

The captain did mention him in the despatches! It was always said he asked that he might be pardoned. He wrote a special letter to the Secretary of War. But nothing ever came of it. As I said, that was about the time when they began to ignore the whole transaction at Washington, and when Nolan's imprisonment began to carry itself on because there was nobody to stop it without any new orders from home.

I have heard it said that he was with Porter when he took possession of the Nukahiwa Islands? Not this Porter, you know, but old Porter, his father, Essex Porter,—that is, the old Essex Porter, not this Essex. As an artillery officer, who had seen service in the West, Nolan knew more about fortifications, embrasures, ravelins, stockades? and all that, than any of them did; and he worked with a right good-will in fixing that battery all right. I have always thought it was a pity Porter did not leave him in command there with Gamble. That would have settled all the question about his punishment. We should have kept the islands, and at this moment we should have one station in the Pacific Ocean. Our French friends, too, when they wanted this little watering-place, would have found it was preoccupied. But Madison and the Virginians, of course, flung all that away.

All that was near fifty years ago. If Nolan was thirty then, he must have been near eighty when he died. He looked sixty when he was forty. But he never seemed to me to change a hair afterwards. As I imagine his life, from what I have seen and heard of it, he must have been in every sea, and yet almost never on land. He must have known, in a formal way, more officers in our service than any man living knows. He told me once, with a grave smile, that no man in the world lived so methodical a life as he. " You know the boys say I am the Iron Mask, and you know how busy he was." He said it did not do for any one to try to read all the time, more than to do anything else all the time; but that he read just five hours a day. "Then," he said, " I keep up my note-books, writing in them at such and such hours from what I have been reading; and I include in these my scrap-books." These were very curious indeed. He had six or eight, of different subjects. There was one of History, one of Natural Science, one which he called " Odds and Ends." But they were not merely books of extracts from newspapers. They had bits of plants and ribbons, shells tied on, and carved scraps of bone and wood which he had taught the men to cut for him, and they were beautifully illustrated. He drew admirably. He had some of the funniest drawings there, and some of the most pathetic, that I have ever seen in my life.    I wonder who will have Nolan's scrap-books.

Well, he said his reading and his notes were his profession, and that they took five hours and two hours respectively of each day. "Then," said he, " every man should have a diversion as well as a profession. My Natural History is my diversion." That took two hours a day more.    The men used to bring him birds and fish, but on a long cruise he had to satisfy himself with centipedes and cockroaches and such small game.    He was the only naturalist I ever met who knew anything about the habits of the house-fly and the mosquito.    All those people can tell you whether they are *Lepidop-tera* or *Steptopotera*[1]*;* but as for telling how you can get rid of them, or how they get away from you when you strike them,— why Linnæus knew as little of that as John Foy[2] the idiot did.    These nine hours made Nolan's regular daily "occupation."    The rest of the time he talked or walked.    Till he grew very old, he went aloft a great deal.    He always kept up his

exercise; and i never heard that he was ill.    If
any other man was ill, he was the kindest nurse
in the world; and he knew more than half the
surgeons do.    Then if anybody was sick or
died, or if the captain wanted him to, on any
other occasion, he was always ready to read
prayers.    I have said that he read beautifully.

My own acquaintance with Philip Nolan
began six or eight years after the War, on my
first voyage after I was appointed a midshipman.    It was in the first days after our Slave-
Trade treaty,¹ while the Reigning House, which
was still the House of Virginia, had still a sort
of sentimentalism about the suppression of the
horrors of the Middle Passage,² and something
was sometimes done that way.    We were in
the South Atlantic on that business.    From
the time I joined, I believe I thought Nolan
was a sort of lay chaplain,— a chaplain with a
blue coat.    I never asked about him.    Everything in the ship was strange to me.    I knew it
was green to ask questions, and I suppose I
thought there was a " Plain-Buttons " on every
ship.    We had him to dine in our mess once a
week, and the caution was given that on that
day nothing was to be said about home.    But if
they had told us not to say anything about the
planet Mars or the Book of Deuteronomy, I
should not have asked why; there were a great

many things which seemed to me to have as
little reason.  I first came to understand anything about " the man without a country " one
day when we overhauled a dirty little schooner
which had slaves on board.  An officer was
sent to take charge of her, and, after a few
minutes, he sent back his boat to ask that some
one might be sent him who could speak Portuguese.  We were all looking over the rail when
the message came, and we all wished we could
interpret, when the captain asked who spoke
Portuguese.  But none of the officers did; and
just as the captain was sending forward to ask
if any of the people could, Nolan stepped out
and said he should be glad to interpret, if the
captain wished, as he understood the language.
The captain thanked him, fitted out another
boat with him, and in this boat it was my luck
to go.

When we got there, it was such a scene as
you seldom see, and never want to.  Nastiness
beyond account, and chaos run loose in the
midst of the nastiness.  There were not a great
many of the negroes; but by way of making
what there were understand that they were
free, Vaughan had had their hand-cuffs and
ankle-cuffs knocked off, and, for convenience'
sake, was putting them upon the rascals of the
schooner's crew.  The negroes were, most of

them, out of the hold, and swarming all round
the dirty deck, with a central throng surround-
ing Vaughan and addressing him in every dialect, and *patois*[1] of a dialect, from the Zulu click
up to the Parisian of Beledeljereed.[2]

As we came on deck, Vaughan looked down
from a hogshead, on which he had mounted in
desperation, and said : —

"For God's love, is there anybody who can
make these wretches understand something?
The men gave them rum, and that did not quiet
them.   I knocked that big fellow down twice,
and that did not soothe him.   And then I talked
Choctaw[3] to all of them together; and I'll be
hanged if they understand that as well as they
understand the English."

Nolan said he could speak Portuguese, and
one or two fine-looking Kroomen[4] were dragged
out, who, as it had been found already, had
worked for the Portuguese on the coast at Fernando Po.[5]

"Tell them they are free," said Vaughan;
"and tell them that these rascals are to be
hanged as soon as we can get rope enough."

Nolan "put them into Spanish," — that is, he
explained it in such Portuguese as the Kroomen
could understand, and they in turn to such of
the negroes as could understand them.   Then
there was such a yell of delight, clinching of

fists, leaping and dancing, kissing of Nolan's
feet, and a general rush made to the hogshead
by way of spontaneous worship of Vaughan, as
the *deus ex machina*[1] of the occasion.

"Tell them," said Vaughan, well pleased,
" that I will take them all to Cape Palmas?"

This did not answer so well.   Cape Palmas
was practically as far from the homes of most
of them as New Orleans or Rio Janeiro was;
that is, they would be eternally separated from
home there.   And their interpreters, as we
could understand, instantly said : "*Ah, non
Palmas*," and began to propose infinite other
expedients in most voluble language.   Vaughan
was rather disappointed at this result of his lib-
erality, and asked Nolan eagerly what they said.
The drops stood on poor Nolan's white forehead,
as he hushed the men down, and said : ─

" He says, ' Not Palmas.'   He says, ' Take us
home, take us to our own country, take us to our
own house, take us to our own pickaninnies and
our own women.'   He says he has an old father
and mother who will die if they do not see him.
And this one says he left his people all sick, and
paddled down to Fernando to beg the white
doctor to come and help them, and that these
devils caught him in the bay just in sight of
home, and that he had never seen anybody from
home since then.   And this one says," choked

out Nolan, "that he has not heard a word from his home in six months, while he has been locked up in an infernal barracoon."

Vaughan always said he grew gray himself while Nolan struggled through this interpretation. I, who did not understand anything of the passion involved in it, saw that the very elements were melting with fervent heat, and that something was to pay somewhere. Even the negroes themselves stopped howling, as they saw Nolan's agony, and Vaughan's almost equal agony of sympathy. As quick as he could get words, he said : —

"Tell them yes, yes, yes ; tell them they shall go to the Mountains of the Moon[1] if they will. If I sail the schooner through the Great White Desert[2] they shall go home!"

And after some fashion Nolan said so. And then they all fell to kissing him again, and wanted to rub his nose with theirs.

But he could not stand it long; and getting Vaughan to say he might go back, he beckoned me down into our boat. As we lay back in the stern-sheets and the men gave way, he said to me: "Youngster, let that show you what it is to be without a family, without a home, and without a country. And if you are ever tempted to say a word or to do a thing that shall put a bar between you and your family, your home, and your country, pray God in his mercy to take you that instant home to his own heaven. Stick by your family, boy; forget you have a self, while you do everything for them.    Think of your home, boy; write and send, and talk about it.    Let it be nearer and nearer to your thought, the farther you have to travel from it; and rush back to it, when you are free, as that poor black slave is doing now.    And for your country, boy," and the words rattled in his throat, " and for that flag," and he pointed to the ship, " never dream a dream but of serving her as she bids you, though the service carry you through a thousand hells.    No matter what happens to you, no matter who flatters you or who abuses you, never look at another flag, never let a night pass but you pray God to bless that flag.    Remember, boy, that behind all these men you have to do with, behind officers, and government, and people even, there is the Country Herself, your Country, and that you belong to Her as you belong to your own mother.    Stand by Her, boy, as you would stand by your mother, if those devils there had got hold of her today ! "

I was frightened to death by his calm, hard passion; but I blundered out, that I would, by all that was holy, and that I had never thought of doing anything else.    He hardly seemed to

hear me; but he did, almost in a whisper, say:
"O, if anybody had said so to me when I was
of your age!"

I think it was this half-confidence of his,
which I never abused, for I never told this
story till now, which afterward made us great
friends.  He was very kind to me.  Often he
sat up, or even got up, at night, to walk the
deck with me, when it was my watch.  He explained to me a great deal of my mathematics,
and I owe to him my taste for mathematics.
He lent me books, and helped me about my
reading.  He never alluded so directly to his
story again; but from one and another officer
I have learned, in thirty years, what I am telling.  When we parted from him in St. Thomas'
harbor, at the end of our cruise, I was more
sorry than I can tell.  I was very glad to meet
him again in 1830; and later in life, when I
thought I had some influence in Washington, I
moved heaven and earth to have him discharged.
But it was like getting a ghost out of prison.
They pretended there was no such man, and
never was such a man.  They will say so at
the Department now!  Perhaps they do not
know.  It will not be the first thing in the service of which the Department appears to know
nothing!

There is a story that Nolan met Burr once

on one of our vessels, when a party of Americans came on board in the Mediterranean. But this I believe to be a lie; or, rather it is a myth, *ben trovato*, involving a tremendous blowing-up with which he sunk Burr,— asking him how he liked to be "without a country." But it is clear from Burr's life that nothing of the sort could have happened; and I mention this only as an illustration of the stories which get a-going where there is the least mystery at bottom.

So poor Philip Nolan had his wish fulfilled. I know but one fate more dreadful; it is the fate reserved for those men who shall have one day to exile themselves from their country because they have attempted her ruin, and shall have at the same time to see the prosperity and honor to which she rises when she has rid herself of them and their iniquities. The wish of poor Nolan, as we all learned to call him, not because his punishment was too great, but because his repentance was so clear, was precisely the wish of every Bragg[2] and Beauregard[3] who broke a soldier's oath two years ago, and of every Maury and Barron[4] who broke a sailor's. I do not know how often they have repented. I do know that they have done all that in them lay that they might have no country,— that all the honors, associations, memories, and hopes which belong to "country" might be broken up into little shreds and distributed to the winds. I know, too, that their punishment, as they vegetate through what is left of life to them in wretched Boulognes and Leicester Squares, where they are destined to upbraid each other till they die, will have all the agony of Nolan's, with the added pang that every one who sees them will see them to despise and to execrate them. They will have their wish, like him.

For him, poor fellow, he repented of his folly, and then, like a man, submitted to the fate he had asked for. He never intentionally added to the difficulty or delicacy of the charge of those who had him in hold. Accidents would happen; but they never happened from his fault. Lieutenant Truxton told me, that, when Texas was annexed, there was a careful discussion among the officers, whether they should get hold of Nolan's handsome set of maps, and cut Texas out of it,— from the map of the world and the map of Mexico. The United States had been cut out when the atlas was bought for him. But it was voted, rightly enough, that to do this would be virtually to reveal to him what had happened, or, as Harry Cole said, to make him think Old Burr had succeeded. So it was from no fault of Nolan's that a great botch happened at my own table,

when, for a short time, I was in command of
the George Washington corvette, on the South
American Station.   We were lying in the La
Plata¹, and some of the officers, who had been
on shore, and had just joined again, were enter-
taining us with accounts of their misadventures
in riding the half-wild horses of Buenos Ayres².
Nolan was at table, and was in an unusually
bright and talkative mood.   Some story of a
tumble reminded him of an adventure of his
own,'when he was catching wild horses in Texas
with his adventurous cousin at a time when he
must have been quite a boy.   He told the story
with a good deal of spirit,— so much so, that
the silence which often follows a good story
hung over the table for an instant, to be broken
by Nolan himself.   For he asked perfectly unconsciously : —

"Pray, what has become of Texas ?   After
the Mexicans got their independence, I thought
that province of Texas would come forward very
fast.   It is really one of the finest regions on
earth ; it is the Italy of this continent.   But I
have not seen or heard a word of Texas for near
twenty years."

There were two Texan officers at the table.
The reason he had never heard of Texas was
that Texas and her affairs had been painfully
cut out of his newspapers since Austin³ began

his settlements; so that, while he read of Honduras[1] and Tamaulipas,[2] and, till quite lately, of
California,— this virgin province, in which his
brother had travelled so far, and, I believe, had
died, had ceased to be to him.   Waters and
Williams, the two Texas men, looked grimly at
each other, and tried not to laugh.   Edward
Morris had his attention attracted by the third
link in the chain of the captain's chandelier.
Watrous was seized with a convulsion of sneez-
ing.   Nolan himself saw that something was to
pay, he did not know what.   And I, as master
of the feast, had to say, —

"Texas is out of the map, Mr. Nolan.   Have
you seen Captain Back's curious account of Sir
Thomas Roe's[3] Welcome ? "

After that cruise I never saw Nolan again.   I
wrote to him at least twice a year, for in that
voyage we became even confidentially intimate;
but he never wrote to me.   The other men
tell me that in those fifteen years he *aged*
very fast, as well he might indeed, but that he
was still the same gentle, uncomplaining, silent
sufferer that he ever was, bearing as best he
could his self-appointed punishment, — rather
less social, perhaps, with new men whom he did
not know, but more anxious, apparently, than
ever to serve and befriend and teach the boys,
some of whom fairly seemed to worship him.

And now it seems the dear old fellow is dead. He has found a home at last, and a country.

Since writing this, and while considering whether or no I would print it, as a warning to the young Nolans and Vallandighams[1] and Tatnalls[2] of today of what it is to throw away a country, I have received from Danforth, who is on board the Levant, a letter which gives an account of Nolan's last hours. It removes all my doubts about telling this story.

To understand the first words of the letter, the non-professional reader should remember that after 1817, the position of every officer who had Nolan in charge was one of the greatest delicacy. The government had failed to renew the order of 1807 regarding him. What was a man to do ? Should he let him go ? What, then, if he were called to account by the Department for violating the order of 1807 ? Should he keep him ? What, then, if Nolan should be liberated some day, and should bring an action for false imprisonment or kidnapping against every man who had had him in charge ? I urged and pressed this upon Southard, and I have reason to think that other officers did the same thing. But the Secretary always said, as they so often do at Washington, that there were no special orders to give, and that we must act

on our own judgment. That means, " If you
succeed, you will be sustained; if you fail, you
will be disavowed." Well, as Danforth says,
all that is over now, though I do not know but
I expose myself to a criminal prosecution on
the evidence of the very revelation I am
making.

Here is the letter: —

"LEVANT, 2° 2′ S. AT 131° W.

" DEAR FRED: — I try to find heart and life
to tell you that it is all over with dear old Nolan.
I have been with him on this voyage more than
I ever was, and I can understand wholly now
the way in which you used to speak of the dear
old fellow.   I could see that he was not strong,
but I had no idea the end was so near.   The
doctor has been watching him very carefully,
and yesterday morning came to me and told me
that Nolan was not so well, and had not left his
state-room, — a thing I never remember before.
He had let the doctor come and see him as he
lay there, — the first time the doctor had been
in the state-room, — and he said he should like
to see me.   O dear! do you remember the
mysteries we boys used to invent about his
room, in the old Intrepid days?   Well, I went
in, and there, to be sure, the poor fellow lay in
his berth, smiling pleasantly as he gave me his

hand, but looking very frail.    I could not help a glance round, which showed me what a little shrine he had made of the box he was lying in. The stars and stripes were triced up above and around a picture of Washington, and he had painted a majestic eagle, with lightnings blazing from his beak and his foot just clasping the whole globe, which his wings overshadowed. The dear old boy saw my glance, and said, with a sad smile, 'Here, you see, I have a country!' And then he pointed to the foot of his bed, where I had not seen before a great map of the United States, as he had drawn it from memory, and which he had there to look upon as he lay. Quaint, queer old names were on it, in large letters: 'Indiana Territory,' 'Mississippi Territory,' and 'Louisiana Territory,' as I suppose our fathers learned such things; but the old fellow had patched in Texas, too; he had carried his western boundary all the way to the Pacific, but on that shore he had defined nothing.

"'O Danforth,' he said, 'I know I am dying. I cannot get home.   Surely you will tell me something now? — Stop! stop!   Do not speak till I say what I am sure you know, that there is not in this ship, that there is not in America, — God bless her! — a more loyal man than I. There cannot be a man who loves the old flag as I do, or prays for it as I do, or hopes for it as I

do.   There are thirty-four stars in it now, Danforth.   I thank God for that, though I do not
know what their names are.   There has never
been one taken away : I thank God for that.   I
know by that that there has never been any successful Burr.   O Danforth, Danforth,' he sighed
out, ' how like a wretched night's dream a boy's
idea of personal fame or of separate sovereignty
seems, when one looks back on it after such a
life as mine !   But tell me, — tell me something,
— tell me everything, Danforth, before I die ! '

   " Ingham, I swear to you that I felt like a
monster that I had not told him everything
before.   Danger or no danger, delicacy or no
delicacy, who was I, that I should have been
acting the tyrant all this time over this dear,
sainted old man, who had years ago expiated, in
his whole manhood's life, the madness of a boy's
treason ?   ' Mr. Nolan,' said I, ' I will tell you
everything you ask about.   Only, where shall I
begin ? '

   " O the blessed smile that crept over his white
face !  and he pressed my hand and said, ' God
bless you ! '  ' Tell me their names,' he said, and
he pointed to the stars on the flag.   ' The last
I know is Ohio.   My father lived in Kentucky.
But I have guessed Michigan and Indiana and
Mississippi, — that was where Fort Adams is, —
they make twenty.   But where are your other

"'I WILL TELL YOU EVERYTHING YOU ASK ABOUT.'"

fourteen? You have not cut up any of the old ones, I hope?'

"Well, that was not a bad text, and I told him the names in as good order as I could, and he bade me take down his beautiful map and draw them in as I best could with my pencil. He was wild with delight about Texas, told me how his cousin died there; he had marked a gold cross near where he supposed his grave was; and he had guessed at Texas. Then he was delighted as he saw California and Oregon; — that, he said, he had suspected partly, because he had never been permitted to land on that shore, though the ships were there so much. ' And the men,' said he, laughing, ' brought off a good deal besides furs.' Then he went back — heavens, how far! — to ask about the Chesapeake, and what was done to Barron for surrendering her to the Leopard, and whether Burr ever tried again, — and he ground his teeth with the only passion he showed. But in a moment that was over, and he said, ' God forgive me, for I am sure I forgive him.' Then he asked about the old war, — told me the true story of his serving the gun the day we took the Java¹,— asked about dear old David Porter, as he called him. Then he settled down more quietly, and very happily, to hear me tell in an hour the history of fifty years.

"How I wished it had been somebody who knew something! But I did as well as I could. I told him of the English war. I told him about Fulton[1] and the steamboat beginning. I told him about old Scott[2], and Jackson[3]; told him all I could think of about the Mississippi, and New Orleans, and Texas, and his own old Kentucky. And do you think, he asked who was in command of the 'Legion of the West.' I told him it was a very gallant officer named Grant[4], and that, by our last news, he was about to establish his headquarters at Vicksburg. Then, 'Where was Vicksburg?' I worked that out on the map; it was about a hundred miles, more or less, above his old Fort Adams; and I thought Fort Adams must be a ruin now. 'It must be at old Vick's plantation, at Walnut Hills,' said he: 'well, that is a change!'

"I tell you, Ingham, it was a hard thing to condense the history of half a century into that talk with a sick man. And I do not now know what I told him, — of emigration, and the means of it, — of steamboats, and railroads, and telegraphs, — of inventions, and books, and literature, — of the colleges, and West Point, and the Naval School[5], — but with the queerest interruptions that ever you heard. You see it was Robinson Crusoe asking all the accumulated questions of fifty-six years!

" I remember he asked, all of a sudden, who was President now; and when I told him, he asked if Old Abe was General Benjamin Lincoln's son. He said he met old General Lincoln, when he was quite a boy himself, at some Indian treaty. I said no, that Old Abe was a Kentuckian like himself, but I could not tell him of what family; he had worked up from the ranks. 'Good for him!' cried Nolan; 'I am glad of that. As I have brooded and wondered, I have thought our danger was in keeping up those regular successions in the first families.' Then I got talking about my visit to Washington. I told him of meeting the Oregon Congressman, Harding; I told him about the Smithsonian, and the Exploring Expedition; I told him about the Capitol, and the statutes for the pediment, and Crawford's Liberty, and Greenough's Washington: Ingham, I told him everything I could think of that would show the grandeur of his country and its prosperity; but I could not make up my mouth to tell him a word about this infernal Rebellion!

" And he drank it in, and enjoyed it as I cannot tell you. He grew more and more silent, yet I never thought he was tired or faint. I gave him a glass of water, but he just wet his lips, and told me not to go away. Then he asked me to bring the Presbyterian 'Book of

Public Prayer,' which lay there, and said, with a
smile that it would open at the right place,—
and so it did.   There was his double red mark
down the page; and I knelt down and read, and
he repeated with me, 'For ourselves and our
country, O gracious God, we thank Thee, that,
notwithstanding our manifold transgressions for
Thy holy laws, Thou hast continued to us Thy
marvellous kindness,' — and so to the end of
that thanksgiving.   Then he turned to the end
of the same book, and I read the words more
familiar to me: 'Most heartily we beseech Thee
with Thy favor to behold and bless Thy servant,
the President of the United States, and all others in authority,' — and the rest of the Episco-
pal collect.   'Danforth,' said he, 'I have repeated
those prayers night and morning, it is now fifty-
five years.'   And then he said he would go to
sleep.   He bent me down over him and kissed
me; and he said, 'Look in my Bible, Danforth,
when I am gone.'   And I went away.

   "But I had no thought it was the end.   I
thought he was tired and would sleep.   I knew
he was happy and I wanted him to be alone.

   "But in an hour, when the doctor went in
gently, he found Nolan had breathed his life
away with a smile.   He had something pressed
close to his lips.   It was his father's badge of
the Order of the Cincinnati.

"We looked in his Bible, and there was a slip of paper at the place where he had marked the text: —

"'They desire¹ a country, even a heavenly: wherefore God is not ashamed to be called their God: for he hath prepared for them a city.'

"On this slip of paper he had written: —

"'Bury me in the sea; it has been my home, and I love it. But will not some one set up a stone for my memory at Fort Adams or at Orleans, that my disgrace may not be more than I ought to bear? Say on it: —

"'*In Memory of*

"'PHILIP NOLAN,

"'*Lieutenant in the Army of the United States.*

"'He loved his country as no other man has loved her, but no man deserved less at her hands.'"

# NOTES.

PAGE 1.— 1. This story was written in the summer of 1863. It was first published in The Atlantic Monthly, in December of that year. It first appeared in book form in 1868.

2. *I Suppose:* The narrator of the story is Frederic Ingham, supposed to be a retired officer of the United States Navy.

3. *Corvette:* A war vessel, next in rank below a frigate; a corvette usually carried but one tier of guns.

4. *Mackinaw (Mackinac):* A town on the island of Mackinac, at the northern extremity of Lake Huron. The Jesuits, who were explorers of the country, erected Mission houses.

PAGE 2.— 1. *Madison:* The fourth President of the United States was James Madison (1751-1836). His term of office was from 1809 to 1817.

2. *Esprit de corps:* French. The spirit

of the organization; that is, the spirit of loyalty for the well-being of the organization.

3. *Naval Archives:* The records of the navy; in brief its history as it is made; also the place where naval records are kept.

4. *Ross:* General Robert Ross, commander of the British troops; he sacked the city of Washington in 1814, destroying many public buildings.

PAGE 3.— 1. *Non mi recordo :* Italian, I do not remember.

2. *Young Americans of today:* This is, of course, the aim of the book, to show young Americans what it is to be without a country; hence the story is fiction serving the noblest purpose.

3. *Aaron Burr* (1756-1836): An officer in the American Revolution; Vice-president in Jefferson's administration (first term) from 1801 to 1804. Burr killed the Federal Party leader, Alexander Hamilton, in a duel fought in 1804. He later organized a military expedition with the probable intention of wresting Texas from Spain. He was tried for treason but acquitted.

4. *Fort Massac:* A fort formerly situated north of New Orleans.

5. *Barrack-life:* Barracks (commonly used in the plural) are the buildings in which officers and soldiers live.

PAGE 4.— 1. *Monongahela:* A kind of American whisky.

2. *Hazard:* A game played with dice.

3. *High-low-jack:* A card game.

4. *Bourbon:* A kind of American whisky.

5. *Euchre and Poker:* Card games of a later period than that of this narrative.

6. *Weekly Arguses:* A name intended to designate local newspapers.

7. *Canebrake:* A thicket of canes.

PAGE 5.— 1. *Jefferson:* Thomas Jefferson was a Virginian and the men he gathered about him are here alluded to as the House of Virginia.

2. *Break on the Wheel:* A mode of punishment employed in the middle ages to force confession of guilt.

3. *Clarences of the then House of York:* In order to fortify himself and to increase his power, Edward IV, first English sovereign of the House of York, put his brother, the Duke of Clarence, to death.

4. *Puget Sound:* Off the coast of the State of Washington.

5. *Fort Adams:* Situated on the Mississippi and in the south-western part of the State of Mississippi.

6. *Court-martials:* Military courts for those accused of military offenses.

PAGE 6.— 1. *Colonel Morgan:* All characters of the story, with the exception of Aaron Burr, are fictitious.

2. *"Spanish plot," "Orleans plot:"* Plots designed to take forcibly from Spain parts of her dominion in North America. Texas and nearly all the country west of the Mississippi belonged to Spain before 1800.

3. *Vera Cruz* (true cross): A city on the east coast of Mexico and the principal city of the state of the same name.

PAGE 7.— 1. *But once again:* Thus the author enlists the reader's attention and stimulates his interest.

2. *Benedict Arnold* (1741-1801): Traitor to his country.

3. *"God save King George:"* The sovereign referred to is George IV.

4. *The Court:* That is, the officers of the Court.

5. *Mr. Marshal:* The marshal is the Court officer whose duty it is to execute the orders of the judge.

PAGE 8.—1. *Without day:* Usually expressed in the Latin *sine die*, meaning indefinitely.

2. *That is, if I may believe:* Note how the author casts a doubt upon the preceding statement.

3. *Crowninshield:* Benjamin W. Crowninshield was Secretary of the Navy from 1814 to 1818.

PAGE 9.—1. *Tingey:* Thomas Tingey, born in London, served in the British Navy. Subsequently, he came to America and entered the United States Navy. He was placed in charge of the United States Navy Yard in 1804.

2. *Etiquette:* Here meaning the prescribed mode of conduct.

PAGE 10.—1. *Quarters:* Place of residence.

2. *Rations:* The fixed daily allowance of provisions (food) for a sailor or soldier.

PAGE 12.—1. *Sentinel:* A soldier on guard.

2. *Alexandria:* A seaport of Egypt, founded by Alexander the Great.

3. *Cairo:* The capital of Egypt, situated on the Nile.

4. *"Dons:"* The name applied to Spanish gentlemen; hence, as used here, a title of respect.

PAGE 13.—1. *Hesiod:* A Greek poet (c.) 735 B. C.

    2. *Canning's speeches:* George Canning was an English statesman and orator (1770-1827); he was Prime Minister in 1827.

    3. *Packet:* The original meaning is a small package or bundle. Hence, a vessel employed to carry despatches, mails, goods and packages.

PAGE 14.—1. *"Lay of the Last Minstrel:"* Poem by Sir Walter Scott, published in 1805.

    2. *"The Tempest:"* A play by Shakespeare. In Act I, Scene 2, Ariel says:

>                Safely in harbor
> Is the King' ship . . .
>
> .    .    .    .    .
>
> From the still-vexed Bermoothes, there she's hid.

    3. *Border chivalry:* The warfare waged on the boundary between England and Scotland by the Border Knights.

PAGE 16.—1. *Braggadocio:* To boast, to swagger; A character in Spenser's Faerie Queen.

    2. *Flechier's sermons:* Esprit Fléchier (1632-1710), a noted French orator. He became Bishop of Nimes.

    3. *Windward Islands:* The Lesser Antilles, an island group of the West Indies extending from Porto Rico to Trinidad.

4. *Salt junk:* The sailor's name for salted meat.

5. *Rendezvous:* A meeting-place.

PAGE 18.—1. *Bevy:* A company, especially of ladies.

2. *Perhaps:* Note the touch of uncertainty introduced by this word.

3. *Lady Hamilton:* Wife of Sir William Hamilton, British envoy at Naples. Lady Hamilton was a famous beauty and a noted personage in the social life of her times.

4. *Contretemps:* French, an untoward or awkward occurrence; an embarrassing situation.

5. *Contra-dances:* Dances in which the partners stand in two lines opposite each other. They dance in couples down the center and back to their places.

6. *"The Old Thirteen:"* The thirteen original states of the Union; a term that should not be mentioned in Nolan's presence.

PAGE 20.—1. *Cotillions:* A lively dance. It has no characteristic music.

2. *Vesuvius:* A volcano in Southern Italy near Naples.

3. *"Iron Mask:"* A famous French mystery of the period of Louis XIV.

4. *"Junius:"* The nom-de-plume of the

writer of a series of letters, published
in England in the paper known as the
Public Advertiser in 1768 and after.
The letters discussed political matters
and were directed against the
ministry.

PAGE 21.—1. *Libel on Thomas Jefferson:* Letters
directed against Thomas Jefferson and
written by Alexander Hamilton.

PAGE 22.—1. *Raw hands:* Inexperienced men.

PAGE 23.—1. *Despatches:* The commanders' account of the engagement sent to the
Naval Department at Washington.

2. *Nukahiwa Islands:* The Marquesas
Islands in the southern Pacific, taken
by Admiral David Porter in 1813.

3. *Embrasures, ravelins, stockades:* Tech-
nical terms in the art of fortification.

PAGE 24.—1. *Madison and the Virginians:* Madison
and his party did not believe in terri-
torial expansion, that is, in colonial
possessions.

PAGE 25.—1. *Lepidoptera or Steptopotera:* Greek
names for varieties of insects. The
former include the moths, the latter
the butterflies.

2. *John Foy:* The idiot boy in the poem
by William Wordsworth.

PAGE 26.—1. *Slave-Trade Treaty:* Referring to the
Article in the Treaty of Ghent (1814)

having to do with the abolition of the slave trade.

2. *Middle Passage:* That portion of the Atlantic Ocean lying between the west coast of Africa and the American continent.

PAGE 28.—1. *Patois:* A dialect of the illiterate; a provincial form of speech.

2. *Beledeljereed:* In Northern Africa.

3. *Choctaw:* The speech of that tribe of American Indians who occupied a part of what is now Alabama and Mississippi.

4. *Kroomen:* Negroes of the Liberian coast of Africa.

5. *Fernando Po:* An island off the coast of West Africa.

PAGE 29.—1. *Deus ex machina:* The god of the machine.

2. *Cape Palmas:* On the coast of Liberia, West Africa.

PAGE 30.—1. *Mountains of the Moon:* A range of mountains in Central Africa, formerly supposed to be the place of the source of the Nile.

2. *Great White Desert:* The Desert of Sahara.

PAGE 32.—1. *St. Thomas:* An island of the West Indies, which formerly belonged to Denmark, now to the United States.

PAGE 33.—1. *Ben trovato:* Italian; well imagined, or cleverly invented.

2. *Bragg:* General Braxton Bragg (1815-1876).

3. *Beauregard:* General Pierre G. T. Beauregard (1818-1893). Both were graduates of West Point Military Academy, both served in the Mexican War and both entered the Confederate Army.

4. *Maury and Barron:* Matthew Fontaine Maury and Samuel Barron. United States Naval officers who joined the Confederacy.

PAGE 34.—1. *Boulognes and Leicester Squares:* Popular resorts; the former a seaport of France on the English Channel; the latter a popular amusement center in the West End of London.

2. *Texas was annexed:* In 1845.

PAGE 35.—1. *La Plata:* River of Silver; a South American river flowing into the Atlantic Ocean between Argentina and Uruguay.

2. *Buenos Ayres:* The name of a province of the Argentine Republic and of its capital city, situated on the river La Plata.

3. *Austin:* Moses Austin (1764-1821) was allowed by the Mexican Govern-

ment to establish an American colony in Texas.

PAGE 36.—1. *Honduras:* A Central American republic.

2. *Tamaulipas:* A state of Mexico.

3. *Sir Thomas Roe* (1581-1644): An English ambassador and traveler. His "Welcome" probably refers to his triumphal reception in London on his return from abroad.

PAGE 37.—1. *Vallandighams:* Capt. Clement Laird Vallandigham (1820-1871), a member of the House of Representatives. He attacked Lincoln's administration with such animosity and violence that his arrest was ordered by General Burnside. He was tried and sentenced to imprisonment at Fort Warren.

2. *Tatnalls:* Josiah Tatnall (1795-1871) entered the Confederate Army. He was captain of the Merrimac in its encounter with the Monitor.

PAGE 41.—1. *Java:* A British frigate captured by the Constitution.

PAGE 42.—1. *Fulton:* Robert Fulton (1765-1815), inventor of the steamboat. His boat, the Claremont, made a successful trip from New York to Albany, on the Hudson, in August, 1807.

2. *Scott:* Winfield Scott (1786-1866): became Commander-in-Chief of the Army in 1841.

3. *Jackson:* Andrew Jackson (1765-1845), President of the United States for two terms, 1829-1837.

4. *Grant:* Ulysses S. Grant (1822-1885), eighteenth President of the United States, serving two terms, 1869-1877. He was made General in 1866.

5. *Naval School:* The Naval Academy at Annapolis, Md.

PAGE 43.—1. *Smithsonian:* The Smithsonian Institution at Washington, founded by John Smithson, an English scientist.

2. *Crawford's Liberty:* Thomas Crawford (1814-1857), American sculptor, designed a bronze figure of Liberty, which surmounts the dome of the Capitol in Washington.

3. *Greenough's Washington:* Horatio Greenough (1805-1852); his statue of Washington stands in front of the Capitol.

PAGE 44.—1. *Order of the Cincinnati:* The name Cincinnati is derived from that of the Roman Dictator, Lucius Quinctius Cincinnatus. The association was founded by the officers of the Continental Army.

PAGE 45.—1. *They desire:* Hebrews XI-16, "But now they desire a better country, that is, an heavenly."

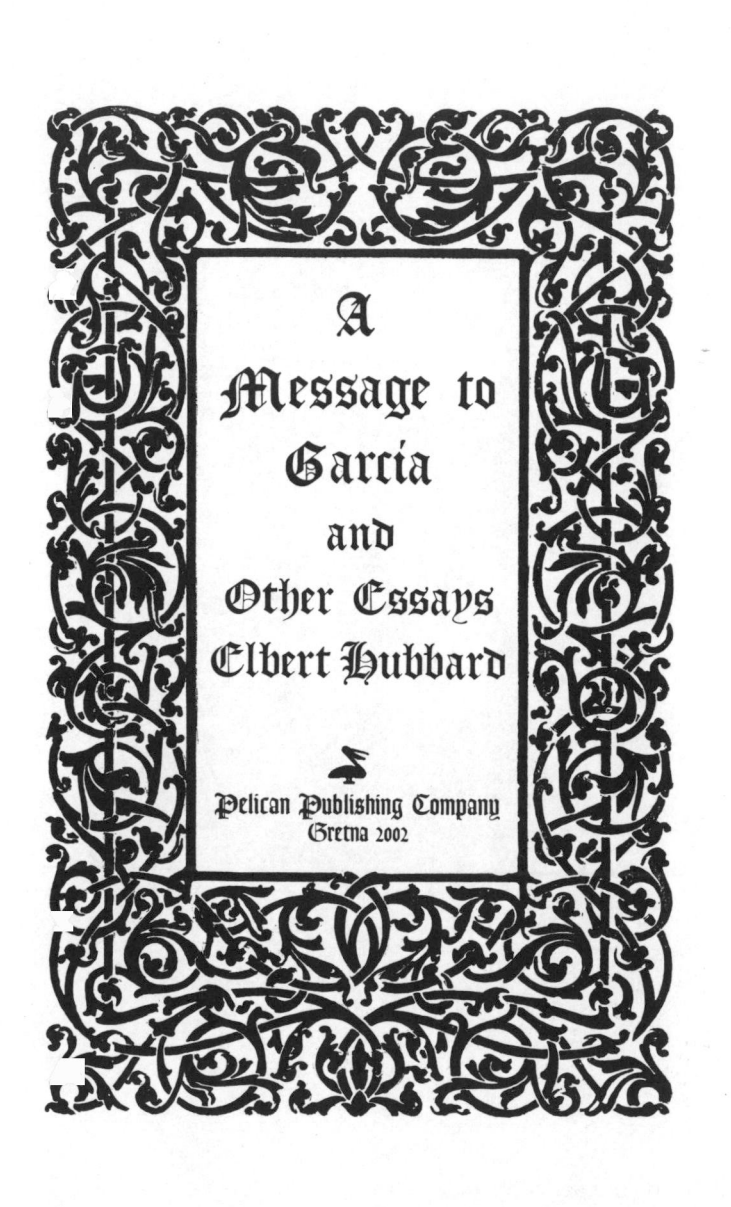

# A
# Message to
# Garcia
# and
# Other Essays
# Elbert Hubbard

Pelican Publishing Company
Gretna 2002

Elbert Hubbard

# A MESSAGE TO GARCIA

## AND OTHER ESSAYS

BY

ELBERT HUBBARD

AUTHORIZED EDITION

PELICAN PUBLISHING COMPANY
Gretna 2002

Copyright © 1916, 1917
By The Roycrofters

First edition, 1916
Second edition, 1917
First Thomas Y. Crowell edition, 1924
First Pelican edition, 2002

**Library of Congress Cataloging-in-Publication Data**

Hale, Edward Everett, 1822-1909.
   The man without a country / Edward Everett Hale. A message to
Garcia / Elbert Hubbard—1st Pelican ed.
      p. cm.
   ISBN 1-56554-453-6 (alk. paper)
   1. Burr Conspiracy, 1805-1807—Fiction. 2. Stateless persons—
Fiction. 3. Soldiers—Fiction. 4. Exiles—Fiction. 5. Rowan, Andrew
Summers. 6. Spanish-American War, 1898. 7. Success. I. Hubbard,
Elbert, 1856-1915. Message to Garcia. 2002. II. Title: Message to
Garcia. III. Title.

PS1772 .M3 2002
813'.4—dc21                                        2002027061

Printed in the United States of America

Published by Pelican Publishing Company, Inc.
1000 Burmaster Street, Gretna, Louisiana 70053

# PUBLISHER'S PREFACE

BY special arrangement with The Roy-crofters we are privileged to republish these papers from the writings of "Fra Elbertus." In the author's "Apologia" he tells the circumstances of writing *A Message to Garcia,* a document which is destined for immortality. The two succeeding papers strike the same high note of responsibility and service.

Elbert Hubbard himself exemplified many of his teachings. He was strong, individual, self-made. Born in 1859, at Bloomington, Illinois, he had only a common-school education, but was an omnivorous reader. His experiment in founding The Roycroft Shop, at East Aurora, New York, devoted to the manufacture of de luxe books, simply carried out a lifetime ambition. Because of his somewhat radical theories and his broad-gauge handling of the labor problem, the experiment was watched elsewhere with much interest. He lived to see it an established success.

Mr. Hubbard toiled early and late.

While he was building the Roycroft Shop he founded and carried on two magazines, *The Philistine* and *The Fra,* and actually wrote a greater part of their contents. But that was not all. He wrote a series of 182 biographies under the general title of "Little Journeys to the Homes of the Great." This work was continued without a break for fourteen years!

Still fearing that he should rust out rather than wear out, he went on the lecture platform, and in his public speaking —thanks to his well-stored mind—he was as great a success as in his writing. His engagements were limited only by his physical endurance.

Few men have equalled him in energy or in output. He was a human dynamo. His production increased with the years, and was cut short by his untimely end, when the *Lusitania* was struck by a German torpedo and went down, May 7, 1915.

Says Franklin K. Lane: "He was a twentieth century Franklin in his application of good sense to modern life." And Thomas A. Edison adds: "He was of big service to me in telling me the things I knew, but which I did not know I knew, until he told me."

# CONTENTS

# A MESSAGE TO GARCIA

# APOLOGIA

THIS literary trifle, *A Message to Garcia,* was written one evening after supper, in a single hour. It was on the Twenty-second of February, Eighteen Hundred Ninety-nine, Washington's Birthday, and we were just going to press with the March *Philistine.* The thing leaped hot from my heart, written after a trying day, when I had been endeavoring to train some rather delinquent villagers to abjure the comatose state and get radioactive.

The immediate suggestion, though, came from a little argument over the teacups, when my boy Bert suggested that Rowan was the real hero of the Cuban War. Rowan had gone alone and done the thing —carried the message to Garcia.

It came to me like a flash! Yes, the boy is right, the hero is the man who does

his work — who carries the message to Garcia.

I got up from the table, and wrote *A Message to Garcia.* I thought so little of it that we ran it in the Magazine without a heading. The edition went out, and soon orders began to come for extra copies of the March *Philistine,* a dozen, fifty, a hundred; and when the American News Company ordered a thousand, I asked one of my helpers which article it was that had stirred up the cosmic dust. "It's the stuff about Garcia," he said.

The next day a telegram came from George H. Daniels, of the New York Central Railroad, thus: "Give price on one hundred thousand Rowan article in pamphlet form—Empire State Express advertisement on back—also how soon can ship."

I replied giving price, and stated we could supply the pamphlets in two years. Our facilities were small and a hundred thousand booklets looked like an awful undertaking.

The result was that I gave Mr. Daniels permission to reprint the article in his own way. He issued it in booklet form in editions of half a million. Two or three of these half-million lots were sent out by Mr. Daniels, and in addition the article was reprinted in over two hundred magazines and newspapers. It has been translated into all written languages.

At the time Mr. Daniels was distributing the *Message to Garcia,* Prince Hilakoff, Director of Russian Railways, was in this country. He was the guest of the New York Central, and made a tour of the country under the personal direction of Mr. Daniels. The Prince saw the little book and was interested in it, more because Mr. Daniels was putting it out in such big numbers, probably, than otherwise.

In any event, when he got home he had the matter translated into Russian, and a copy of the booklet given to every railroad employee in Russia.

Other countries then took it up, and

from Russia it passed into Germany, France, Spain, Turkey, Hindustan and China. During the war between Russia and Japan, every Russian soldier who went to the front was given a copy of the *Message to Garcia.*

The Japanese, finding the booklets in possession of the Russian prisoners, concluded that it must be a good thing, and accordingly translated it into Japanese.

And on an order of the Mikado, a copy was given to every man in the employ of the Japanese Government, soldier or civilian.

Over forty million copies of *A Message to Garcia* have been printed. This is said to be a larger circulation than any other literary venture has ever attained during the lifetime of the author, in all history— thanks to a series of lucky accidents.

*E. H.*

*East Aurora,*
*December* 1, 1913.

# A MESSAGE TO GARCIA

IN all this Cuban business there is one
man stands out on the horizon of my
memory like Mars at perihelion.

When war broke out between Spain and
the United States, it was very necessary
to communicate quickly with the leader of
the Insurgents. Garcia was somewhere
in the mountain fastnesses of Cuba—no
one knew where. No mail or telegraph
message could reach him. The President
must secure his co-operation, and quickly.

What to do!

Someone said to the President, "There
is a fellow by the name of Rowan will find
Garcia for you, if anybody can."

Rowan was sent for and given a letter
to be delivered to Garcia. How the "fellow by the name of Rowan" took the
letter, sealed it up in an oilskin pouch,
strapped it over his heart, in four days

landed by night off the coast of Cuba from an open boat, disappeared into the jungle, and in three weeks came out on the other side of the Island, having traversed a hostile country on foot, and delivered his letter to Garcia—are things I have no special desire now to tell in detail. The point that I wish to make is this: McKinley gave Rowan a letter to be delivered to Garcia; Rowan took the letter and did not ask, "Where is he at?"

By the Eternal! there is a man whose form should be cast in deathless bronze and the statue placed in every college of the land. It is not book-learning young men need, nor instruction about this and that, but a stiffening of the vertebræ which will cause them to be loyal to a trust, to act promptly, concentrate their energies: do the thing—"Carry a message to Garcia."

General Garcia is dead now, but there are other Garcias. No man who has endeavored to carry out an enterprise where many hands were needed, but has been

well-nigh appalled at times by the imbecility of the average man—the inability
or unwillingness to concentrate on a thing
and do it.

Slipshod assistance, foolish inattention,
dowdy indifference, and half-hearted work
seem the rule; and no man succeeds, unless by hook or crook or threat he forces
or bribes other men to assist him; or may-
hap, God in His goodness performs a
miracle, and sends him an Angel of Light
for an assistant.

You, reader, put this matter to a test:
You are sitting now in your office—six
clerks are within call.  Summon any one
and make this request: "Please look in
the encyclopedia and make a brief memorandum for me concerning the life of
Correggio."

Will the clerk quietly say, "Yes, sir,"
and go do the task?

On your life he will not.  He will look
at you out of a fishy eye and ask one or
more of the following questions:

Who was he?

Which encyclopedia?

Where is the encyclopedia?

Was I hired for that?

Don't you mean Bismarck?

What's the matter with Charlie doing it?

Is he dead?

Is there any hurry?

Sha'n't I bring you the book and let you look it up yourself?

What do you want to know for?

And I will lay you ten to one that after you have answered the questions, and explained how to find the information, and why you want it, the clerk will go off and get one of the other clerks to help him try to find Garcia—and then come back and tell you there is no such man. Of course I may lose my bet, but according to the Law of Average I will not.

Now, if you are wise, you will not bother to explain to your "assistant" that Correggio is indexed under the C's, not in the K's, but you will smile very sweetly and say, "Never mind," and go look it up yourself. And this incapacity for inde-

pendent action, this moral stupidity, this infirmity of the will, this unwillingness to cheerfully catch hold and lift—these are the things that put pure Socialism so far into the future. If men will not act for themselves, what will they do when the benefit of their effort is for all?

A first mate with knotted club seems necessary; and the dread of getting "the bounce" Saturday night holds many a worker to his place. Advertise for a stenographer, and nine out of ten who apply can neither spell nor punctuate— and do not think it necessary to.

Can such a one write a letter to Garcia?

"You see that bookkeeper," said the foreman to me in a large factory.

"Yes; what about him?"

"Well, he's a fine accountant, but if I'd send him up town on an errand, he might accomplish the errand all right, and on the other hand, might stop at four saloons on the way, and when he got to Main Street would forget what he had been sent for."

Can such a man be entrusted to carry a message to Garcia?

We have recently been hearing much maudlin sympathy expressed for the "downtrodden denizens of the sweatshop" and the "homeless wanderer searching for honest employment," and with it all often go many hard words for the men in power.

Nothing is said about the employer who grows old before his time in a vain attempt to get frowsy ne'er-do-wells to do intelligent work; and his long, patient striving after "help" that does nothing but loaf when his back is turned. In every store and factory there is a constant weeding-out process going on. The employer is constantly sending away "help" that have shown their incapacity to further the interests of the business, and others are being taken on. No matter how good times are, this sorting continues: only, if times are hard and work is scarce, the sorting is done finer—but out and forever out the incompetent and unworthy go. It is the survival of the fittest. Self-interest

prompts every employer to keep the best
— those who can carry a message to
Garcia.

I know one man of really brilliant parts
who has not the ability to manage a business of his own, and yet who is absolutely
worthless to anyone else, because he carries with him constantly the insane sus-
picion that his employer is oppressing,
or intending to oppress, him. He cannot
give orders, and he will not receive them.
Should a message be given him to take to
Garcia, his answer would probably be,
"Take it yourself!"

Tonight this man walks the streets looking for work, the wind whistling through
his threadbare coat. No one who knows
him dare employ him, for he is a regular
firebrand of discontent. He is impervious
to reason, and the only thing that can
impress him is the toe of a thick-soled
Number Nine boot.

Of course, I know that one so morally
deformed is no less to be pitied than a
physical cripple; but in our pitying let us

drop a tear, too, for the men who are striving to carry on a great enterprise, whose working hours are not limited by the whistle, and whose hair is fast turning white through the struggle to hold in line dowdy indifference, slipshod imbecility, and the heartless ingratitude which, but for their enterprise, would be both hungry and homeless.

Have I put the matter too strongly? Possibly I have; but when all the world has gone a-slumming I wish to speak a word of sympathy for the man who succeeds—the man who, against great odds, has directed the efforts of others, and having succeeded, finds there's nothing in it: nothing but bare board and clothes.    I have carried a dinner-pail and worked for day's wages, and I have also been an employer of labor, and I know there is something to be said on both sides.    There is no excellence, per se, in poverty; rags are no recommendation; and all employers are not rapacious and high-handed, any more than all poor men are virtuous.    My heart

goes out to the man who does his work when the "boss" is away, as well as when he is at home. And the man who, when given a letter for Garcia, quietly takes the missive, without asking any idiotic questions, and with no lurking intention of chucking it into the nearest sewer, or of doing aught else but deliver it, never gets "laid off," nor has to go on a strike for higher wages. Civilization is one long, anxious search for just such individuals. Anything such a man asks shall be granted. He is wanted in every city, town and village—in every office, shop, store and factory. The world cries out for such; he is needed and needed badly—the man who can "Carry a Message to Garcia."

# THE BOY FROM MISSOURI
## VALLEY

# THE BOY FROM MISSOURI
# VALLEY

WELL, it wasn't so very long ago—
only about twenty-three years.

I was foreman of a factory, and he lived
a thousand miles away, at Missouri Valley, Iowa. I was twenty-four, and he was
fourteen. His brother was traveling for
the Firm, and one day this brother showed
me a letter from the lad in Missouri Valley. The missive was so painstaking, so
exact, and revealed the soul of the 'child
so vividly, that I laughed aloud—a laugh
that died away to a sigh.

The boy was beating his wings against
the bars—the bars of Missouri Valley—he
wanted opportunity. And all he got was
unending toil, dead monotony, stupid
misunderstanding, and corn-bread and
molasses.

**There** wasn't love enough in Missouri Valley to go 'round—that was plain. The boy's mother had been of the Nancy Hanks type—worn, yellow and sad—and had given up the fight and been left to sleep her long sleep in a prairie grave on one of the many migrations. The father's ambition had got stuck in the mud, and under the tongue-lash of a strident, strenuous, gee-haw consort, he had run up the white flag.

The boy wanted to come East.

It was a dubious investment—a sort of financial plunge, a blind pool—to send for this buckwheat midget. The fare was thirty-three dollars and fifty cents.

The Proprietor, a cautious man, said that the boy wasn't worth the money. There were plenty of boys—the alleys swarmed with them.

So there the matter rested.

But the lad in Missouri Valley didn't let it rest long. He had been informed that we did not consider him worth thirty-three dollars and fifty cents, so he offered

to split the difference.  He would come for half—he could ride on half-fare—the Railroad Agent at Missouri Valley said that if he bought a half-fare ticket, got on a train, and explained to the conductor and everybody that he was 'leven, goin' on twelve, and stuck to it, it would be all right; and he would not expect any wages until he had paid us back.  He had no money of his own, all he earned was taken from him by the kind folks with whom he lived, and would be until noon of the day he was twenty-one years old.  Did we want to invest sixteen dollars and seventy-five cents in him?

We waxed reckless and sent the money —more than that, we sent a twenty-dollar bill.  We plunged!

In just a week the investment arrived.  He did not advise when he would come, or how.  He came, we saw, he conquered.  Why should he advise of his coming?  He just reported, and his first words were the Duke's motto: "I am here."

He was unnecessarily freckled and curi-

ously small. His legs had the Greek curve
from much horseback riding, herding cat-
tle on the prairies; his hair was the color
of a Tamworth pig; his hands were red;
his wrists bony and briar-scarred. He
carried his shoes in his hands, so as not
to wear out the sidewalk, or because they
aggravated sundry stone-bruises—I don't
know which.

"I am here!" said the lad, and he
planked down on the desk three dollars
and twenty-five cents. It was the change
from the twenty-dollar bill. "Didn't you
have to spend any money on the way
here?" I asked.

"No, I had all I wanted to eat," he
replied, and pointed to a basket that sat
on the floor.

I called in the Proprietor, and we
looked the lad over. We walked around
him twice, gazed at each other, and adjourned to the hallway for consultation.

The boy was not big enough to do a
man's work, and if we set him to work in
the factory with the city boys, they would

surely pick on him and make life for him
very uncomfortable. He had a half-sad
and winsome look that had won from our
hard hearts something akin to pity. He
was so innocent, so full of faith, and we
saw at a glance that he had been over-
worked, underfed—at least misfed—and
underloved. He was different from other
boys—and in spite of the grime of travel,
and the freckles, he was pretty as a
ground-squirrel.

His faith made him whole: he won us.
But why had we brought him to the mis-
erable and dirty city—this grim place of
disillusionment! "He might index the letter-book?" I ventured. "That's it, yes, let
him index the letter-book." So I went
back and got the letter-book. But the
boy's head only come to the top of the
stand-up desk, and when he reached for
the letter-book on the desk he had to grope
for it. I gave him my high-stool, but this
was too low.

"I know what to do," he said. Through
the window that looked from the office to

the shipping-room, he had espied a pile of boxes. "I know what to do!"

In a minute he had placed two boxes end to end, nailed them together, clinched the nails, and carried his improvised high-stool into the office.

"I know what to do!"

And he usually did; and does yet.

We found him a boarding-place with a worthy widow whose children had all grown big and flown. Her house was empty, and so was her mother-heart: she was like that old woman in *Rab,* who was placed on the surgeon's table and given chloroform, and who held to her breast an imaginary child, and crooned a lullaby to a babe, dead thirty years before.

So the boy boarded with the widow and worked in the office.

He indexed the letter-book—he indexed everything. And then he filed everything —letters, bills, circulars. He stamped the letters going out, swept the office, and dusted things that had never been dusted before. He was orderly, alert, active,

cheerful, and the Proprietor said to me one day, "I wonder how we ever got along without that boy from Missouri Valley!"

Six months had passed, and there came a day when one of the workmen intimated to the Proprietor that he better look out for that red-headed office-boy.

Of course, the Proprietor insisted on hearing the rest, and the man then explained that almost every night the boy came back to the office. He had seen him. The boy had a tin box and letter-books in it, and papers, and the Lord knows what not!

Watch him!

The Proprietor advised with me because I was astute—at least he thought I was, and I agreed with him.

He thought Jabesh was at the bottom of it.

Jabesh was our chief competitor. Jabesh had hired away two of our men, and we had gotten three of his. "Jabe," we called him in derision—Jabe had gotten

into the factory twice on pretense of see-
ing a man who wanted to join the Ep-
worth League or Something. We had
ordered him out, because we knew he was
trying to steal our "process." Jabe was
a rogue—that was sure.

Worse than that, Jabe was a Metho-
dist. The Proprietor was a Baptist, and
regarded all Methodists with a prenatal
aversion that swung between fear and contempt. The mere thought of Jabe gave
us gooseflesh. Jabesh was the bugaboo
that haunted our dreams. Our chief
worry was that we would never be able
to save our Bank-Balance alive, for fear
o' Jabe.

"That tarnashun Jabe has hired our office-boy to give him a list of our customers—he is stealing our formulas, I know,"
said the Proprietor. "The cub's pretense
of wanting a key to the factory so he
could sweep out early was really that he
might get in late."

Next day we watched the office-boy.
He surely looked guilty — his freckles

stood out like sunspots, and he was more
bow-legged than ever.

The workman who had given the clue,
on being further interrogated, was sure
he had seen Jabe go by the factory twice
in one evening.

That settled it.

At eight o'clock that night we went
down to the factory.  It was a full mile,
and in an "objectionable" part of the
town.

There was a dim light in the office.  We
peered through the windows, and sure
enough, there was the boy hard at work
writing.  There were several books before
him, a tin box and some papers.  We
waited and watched him copy something
into a letter-book.

We withdrew and consulted.  To con-
front the culprit then and there seemed
the proper thing.  We unlocked the door
and walked softly in.

The boy was startled by our approach,
and still more by our manner.  When the
Proprietor demanded the letter that he

had just written, he began to cry, and then we knew we had him.

The Proprietor took the letter and read it. It was to Jimmy Smith in Missouri Valley. It told all about how the writer was getting on, about the good woman he boarded with, and it told all about me and about the Proprietor. It pictured us as models of virtue, excellence and truth.

But we were not to be put off thus. We examined the letter-book, and alas! it was filled only with news-letters to sundry cousins and aunts. Then we dived to the bottom of the tin box, still in search of things contraband. All we found was a little old Bible, a diary, and some trinkets in the way of lace and a ribbon that had once been the property of the dead Nancy Hanks.

Then we found a Savings-Bank Book, and by the entries saw that the boy had deposited one dollar every Monday morning for eleven weeks. He had been with us for six months, and his pay was two dollars a week and board—we wondered what he had done with the rest!

We questioned the offender at length. The boy averred that he came to the office evenings only because he wanted to write letters and get his 'rithmetic lesson. He would not think of writing his personal letters on our time, and the only reason he wanted to write at the office instead of at home was so he could use the letter-press. He wanted to copy all of his letters—one should be businesslike in all things.

The Proprietor coughed and warned the boy never to let it happen again. We started for home, walking silently but very fast.

The stillness was broken only once, when the Proprietor said: "That con-sarned Jabe! If ever I find him around our factory, I'll tweak his nincompoop nose, that's what I will do."

Twenty-three years! That factory has grown to be the biggest of its kind in America. The red-haired boy from Missouri Valley is its manager. Emerson says, "Every great institution is the lengthened shadow of a single man."

The Savings-Bank Habit came naturally to that boy from Missouri Valley. In a year he was getting six dollars and board, and he deposited four dollars every Monday. In three years this had increased to ten, and some years after, when he became a partner, he had his limit in the Bank. The Savings-Bank Habit is not so bad as the Cab Habit—nor so costly to your thinkery and wallet as the Cigarette Habit.

I have been wage-earner, foreman and employer. I have had a thousand men on my payroll at a time, and I'll tell you this: The man with the Savings-Bank Habit is the one who never gets laid off: he's the one who can get along without you, but you can not get along without him. The Savings-Bank Habit means sound sleep, good digestion, cool judgment and manly independence. The most healthful thing I know of is a Savings-Bank Book—there are no microbes in it to steal away your peace of mind. It is a guarantee of good behavior.

The Missouri Valley boy gets twenty-five thousand a year, they say. It is none too much. Such masterly men are rare; Rockefeller says he has vacancies for eight now, with salaries no object, if they can do the work.

That business grew because the boy from Missouri Valley grew with it, and he grew because the business grew. Which is a free paraphrase from Macaulay, who said that Horace Walpole influenced his age because he was influenced by his age. Jabesh has gone on his Long Occasion, discouraged and whipped by an unappreciative world. Jabe never acquired the Savings-Bank Habit. If he had had the gumption to discover a red-haired boy from Missouri Valley, he might now be sporting an automobile on Delaware Avenue instead of being in Abraham's Bosom.

We shall all be in Abraham's Bosom day after tomorrow; and then I'll explain to Jabesh that no man ever succeeded in a masterly way, excepting as he got level-

headed men with the Savings-Bank Habit to do his work. Blessed is that man who has found somebody to do his work.

There is plenty of iron pyrites, but the Proprietor and I know Pay-Gravel when we see it.

I guess so!

# HELP YOURSELF BY HELPING
THE HOUSE

# HELP YOURSELF BY HELPING THE HOUSE

LITTLE hotels often feature their clerks, while small tailors proudly put forth their cutters. But a big business is built by many earnest men working together for a common end and aim. It is planned by one man, but is carried forward by many.

A steamship is manned by a crew, and no one particular sailor is necessary. You can replace any man in the engine-room of the *Mauretania,* and she will still cross the ocean in less than six days.

In an enterprise that amounts to anything, all transactions should be in the name of the firm, because the firm is more than any one person connected with it. Clerks or salesmen who have private letterheads, and ask customers to send letters to them personally, are on the wrong track.

To lose your identity in the business is

one of the penalties of working for a great institution.  Don't protest—it is no new thing—all big concerns are confronted by the same situation—get in line!  It is a necessity.

If you want to do business individually and in your own name, stay in the country or do business for yourself.

Peanut-stands are individualistic; when the peanut - man goes, the stand also croaks.  Successful corporations are something else.

Of course, the excuse is that, if you send me the order direct, I, knowing you and your needs, can take much better care of your wants than that despised and intangible thing, "the house."  Besides, sending it through the Circumlocution Office takes time.

There is something more to say.  First, long experience has shown that "the saving of time" is exceedingly problematic. For while in some instances a rush order can be gotten off the same night by sending it to an individual, yet when your indi-

vidual has gone fishing, is at the ball-game, or is sick, or else has given up his job and gone with the opposition house, there are great and vexatious delays, dire confusions and a great strain on vocabularies.

This thing of a salesman carrying his trade with him, and considering the customers of the house his personal property, is the thought of only 2 x 4 men. A house must have a certain fixed policy—a reputation for square dealing—otherwise it could not exist at all. It could not even give steady work and good pay to the men who think it would be only a hole in the ground without them.

In the main, the policy of the house is right. Don't acquire the habit of butting in with your stub-end of a will in opposition to the general policy of the house. To help yourself, get in line with your house, stand by it, take pride in it, respect it, uphold it, and regard its interests as yours. The men who do these things become the only ones who are really necessary. They are Top - Notchers, Hundred - Pointers.

The worst about the other plan is that it ruins the man who undertakes it. For a little while, to do a business of your own in the shadow of the big one is beautiful —presents come, personal letters, invitations, favors, is Mr. Johnson in! By and by Johnson gets chesty; he resents it when other salesmen wait on his customers or look after his mail. He begins to plot for personal gain, and the first thing you know he is a plain grafter, at loggerheads with his colleagues, with the interests of the house secondary to his own.

We must grow towards the house, and with it, not away from it. Any policy which lays an employee open to temptation, or tends to turn his head, causing him to lose sight of his own best interests, seizing at a small present betterment, and losing the great advantage of a life's business, is bad. The open cash-drawer, valuable goods lying around not recorded or inventoried, free-and-easy responsibility, good-enough plans, and let-'er-go policies, all tend to ruin men just as surely as do

cigarettes, booze, pasteboards and the races.

The man who thinks he owns "his trade," and threatens to walk out and take other employees and customers with him, is slated to have his dream come true. The manager gives in—the individualist then is sure he is right—the enlarged ego grows, and some day the house simply takes his word for it, and out he goes. The down-and-outer heads off his mail at the Post-Office, and for some weeks embarrasses customers, delays trade and more or less confuses system, but a month or two smooths things out, and he is forgotten absolutely. The steamship plows right along.

Our egotist gets a new job, only to do it all over again if he can. This kind of a man seldom learns. When he gets a job, he soon begins to correspond with rival firms for a better one, with intent to take his "good-will" along.

The blame should go back to the first firm where he was employed, that allowed

him a private letterhead, and let him get filled with the fallacy that he was doing business on his own account, thus losing sight of the great truth that we win through co-operation and not through segregation or separation. The firm's interests are yours; if you think otherwise, you are already on the slide.

The only man who should be given full swing and unlimited power is the one who can neither resign nor run away when the crash comes, but who has to stick and face the deficit, and shoulder the disgrace of failure. All who feel free to hike whenever the weather gets thick would do well to get in line with the policy of the house.

The weak point in Marxian Socialism, is that it plans to divide benefits, but does not say who shall take care of deficits. It relieves everybody of the responsibility of failure and defeat. And just remember this: unless somebody assumes the responsibility of defeat, there will be no benefits to distribute. Also this: that the man who is big enough to be a Somebody is also willing to be a Nobody.